Orca Whale Pod

Julie Murray

abdopublishing.com

Published by Abdo Kids, a division of ABDO, P.O. Box 398166, Minneapolis, Minnesota 55439. Copyright © 2019 by Abdo Consulting Group, Inc. International copyrights reserved in all countries. No part of this book may be reproduced in any form without written permission from the publisher. Abdo Kids Junior™ is a trademark and logo of Abdo Kids.

Printed in the United States of America, North Mankato, Minnesota.

052018

092018

Photo Credits: Glow Images, iStock, Minden Pictures, Science Source, Seapics.com, Shutterstock

Production Contributors: Teddy Borth, Jennie Forsberg, Grace Hansen

Design Contributors: Christina Doffing, Candice Keimig, Dorothy Toth

Library of Congress Control Number: 2017960609

Publisher's Cataloging-in-Publication Data

Names: Murray, Julie, author.
Title: Orca Whale pod / by Julie Murray.
Description: Minneapolis, Minnesota : Abdo Kids, 2019. | Series: Animal groups |
    Includes glossary, index and online resources (page 24).
Identifiers: ISBN 9781532107832 (lib.bdg.) | ISBN 9781532108815 (ebook) |
    ISBN 9781532109300 (Read-to-me ebook)
Subjects: LCSH: Killer Whale--Orca--Juvenile literature. | Animal behavior--Juvenile literature. |
    Social behavior in animals--Juvenile literature. | Animal species--Juvenile literature.
Classification: DDC 599.536--dc23

Table of Contents

Orca Whale Pod 4

Being in a Pod. 22

Glossary. 23

Index 24

Abdo Kids Code. 24

Orca Whale Pod

Orcas are also called killer whales. They live in the ocean.

They live in a group.

It is called a pod.

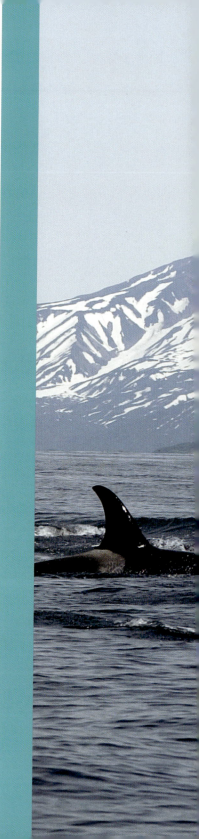

A pod has 5 to 50 orcas.

They are big! They can be 32 feet (9.8 m) long.

They hunt together. They like to eat sea lions.

The pod **protects** its young.

Orcas talk. They make **clicking** sounds. They whistle too.

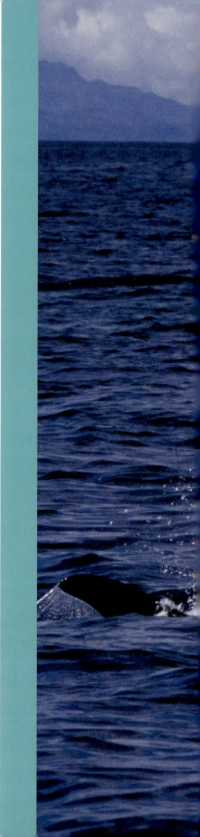

Each pod has its own sound.

Some pods stay in one area.

Some travel for many miles.

Being in a Pod

5 to 50 in a pod

hunt together

protect the young

talk to each other

Glossary

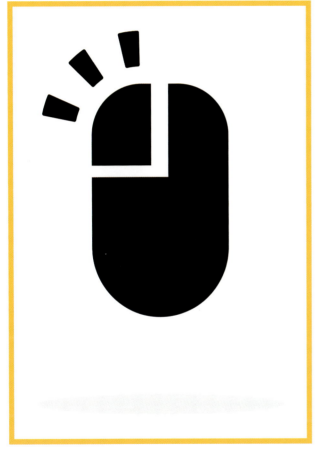

click
a short, sharp sound.

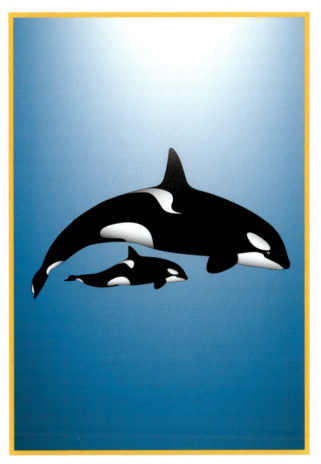

protect
to keep safe from harm.

Index

calf 14

communication 16, 18

food 12

hunt 12

members 8

ocean 4

sea lions 12

size 10

sounds 16, 18

travel 20

Visit **abdokids.com** and use this code to access crafts, games, videos, and more!

Abdo Kids Code:
AOK7832